SPIRITUAL HEALING

Heal Your Life, Cleanse Your Body, Clear Your Mind, and Increase Mindfulness with Guided Meditation

Sarah Rowland

Copyright © **2017 by** Sarah Rowland

All rights reserved. No part of this book may be reproduced or transmitted in any form or by any means, electronic or mechanical, including photocopying, recording or by any information storage and retrieval system without written permission of the publisher, except for the inclusion of brief quotations in a review.

TABLE OF CONTENTS

INTRODUCTION 1

Chapter 1 *What Is The Spirit?* 2

Chapter 2 *What Is Spiritual Healing?* 7

Chapter 3 *Power Of Spiritual Healing* 13

Chapter 4 *The Third Eye* 19

Chapter 5 *Finding Happiness Through Your Spirit* 24

Chapter 6 *Lifting The Spirit With Prayer* 29

Chapter 7 *Visualization And Guided Imagery* 34

Chapter 8 *Radionics, Using Waves Of Energy As Healing* 40

Chapter 9 *Bodhicitta* 45

Chapter 10 *Channeling* 49

Chapter 11 *Color Healing* 54

Chapter 12 *Meditation-Methods And Benefits To Connecting To Spirit* 59

Chapter 13 *5-Minute Meditation* 69

Chapter 14 *15-Minute Meditation* 71

Chapter 15 *30-Minute Meditation* 75

Conclusion 80

INTRODUCTION

Congratulations on downloading your personal copy of *Spiritual Healing: Heal Your Life, Cleanse Your Body, Clear Your Mind, and Increase Mindfulness with Guided Meditation*. Thank you for doing so.

The following chapters will discuss some of the many ways to heal a broken inner spirit through self-help.

You will discover how important getting back in touch with your inner spirit is to increase your energy and improve your overall quality of life.

The final chapter will explore the benefits of healing meditation with guided meditation sessions.

There are plenty of books on this subject on the market, thanks again for choosing this one! Every effort was made to ensure it is full of as much useful information as possible. Please enjoy!

CHAPTER 1
What Is The Spirit?

The idea of the word 'spirit' is just that: an idea. Your spirit cannot be defined, as it is a physically intangible presence that we cannot see or touch, but we can certainly feel it. Everyone's individual perception of their own spirit will be different, as the way they interact and view it will be a personal experience.

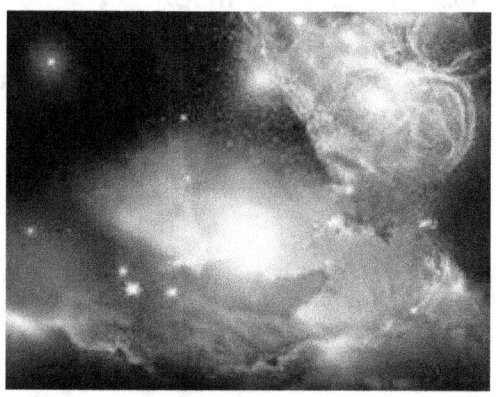

To put some sort of definition on it, our spirit is the essence of ourselves, the energy equivalent to our physical body here on this earth. While our bodies seem to move and are technically alive, it is the true energy of the spirit that drives the physical body forward. The spirit is what will go on once our earthly body has breathed its last breath. It is hard to imagine what will become of us after death, and it is because we cannot imagine not existing, not thinking, not being aware of our surroundings. Even during sleep, we are aware, dreaming and imagining new things.

Many religions have their own definitions of the spirit and go as far as to name the entire energy system of the universe as a tangible thing, for the sake of simplicity, if we were to guess. You may call it God, Allah, Krishna, Supreme Being, it does not matter. Our brains like to make sense of what it cannot tangibly make sense of, and so putting a name on it can define it.

While there are many ideas about what will happen to our spirits after we go, that is not terribly concerning, as we have plenty of time to spend here on earth first. The more important question is, what are we meant to do in our time here?

To break it down, our spirit and even our bodies are just made of energy. The universe has pushed a mass of molecules together to make our human form, and the energy that drives it is our spirit. Here, we must celebrate our differences, as the universe carefully selected each arrangement of molecules to be uniquely perfect. No two humans are exactly alike.

Our spirit gives us a presence we would not otherwise have. It drives the decisions we make and ultimately molds our personality to become who we are. The energy inside of us is pure and perfect, and everything it does is in line with the energy of the universe. This not only applies to humans, but to all living things on this planet.

Our spiritual energy is connected to the universal energy, and each of us is therefore connected by the same common force. Energy is perfect, intertwining in circles and connecting at all points, swirling around in a beautiful, careful arrangement.

Humans are prone to mimic those around them, building societies and maintaining social contact with others. We learn from each other and do our best to 'fit in'. This doesn't work well, considering the universe meant for us each to be different and perfect for that difference.

The odd thing with humans is, we are too smart for our own good. We have evolved with a brain that is capable of going against the inner spirit, despite its best efforts. For the sake of being normal, we often forgo our spiritual needs for the sake of taking a job, making money and settling down. After all, this is what is expected of a socially normal, successful human. We go against the normal flow of energy down a life path that doesn't jive with our inner spirit. Going against the energy is like trying to drive down the wrong lane of traffic. You are going to be met with resistance.

Modern society has taught us to be vain, self-centered and disrespectful to the earth. We focus on our outward appearance, we do things only for our benefit, despite the suffering of others.

We put the health of our environment and the living things around us for the sake of our petty lives.

While we are generally a bad influence for ourselves, there is still hope to turn it around. Our inner spirit will never go away, and it works tirelessly to get us back to our flow of energy. It gives us signals, loud ones, that we often ignore. You may recognize it as intuition, a gut feeling. It may make you feel stressed in certain situations that you should not have gotten yourself into, like working for a company that is morally irresponsible.

We need to relearn how to listen to our spirit so that we may correct our wayward path. Everything we need to know about the future, and all the guidance we could ever need is right there inside, it is only a matter of listening.

As this spirit is solely made up of energy, it would make sense that our spirit can also be drained of energy. Think of it this way: if your spirit is working as hard as it can to get you on the right path, and if you are truly, of

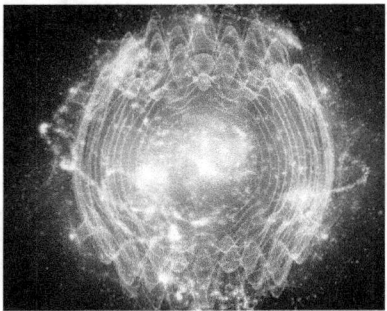

course, working a job you hate, being in relationships that are unfulfilling and abusive, your spirit has a lot of work to do. Imagine being your caretaker. Wouldn't you run out of steam too?

The following chapters in this book will be dedicated to finding different ways to renew and reinvigorate the spirit, as well as to better connect with it. We often let the little signals it gives pass us by, and that is a mistake. Your spiritual intuition sees the big picture from above and can see trouble coming before it even reaches your horizon line. Tapping into this energy can lead you to a happier, more fulfilling and successful life. All you have to do is listen.

CHAPTER 2

What Is Spiritual Healing?

Having a spirit that is entirely made up of energy is a complicated thing. Just like the energy in your home, the power can go out at any given time. While your lights may flicker and your TV show may temporarily be interrupted, a spiritual outage is much more damaging. If your spirit is extinguished, it makes the rest of your life nearly impossible to live, as you no longer have your guidance. The good news is, every spirit has an ember burning, no matter how dim that light.

The most common douser of spiritual light is everyday life. We all get in situations that we don't like, take jobs that we hate to make ends meet, or hang out with people that are a bad influence and don't appreciate us. Anytime we do or say things that are out of spiritual character, our inner self-dims a little inside.

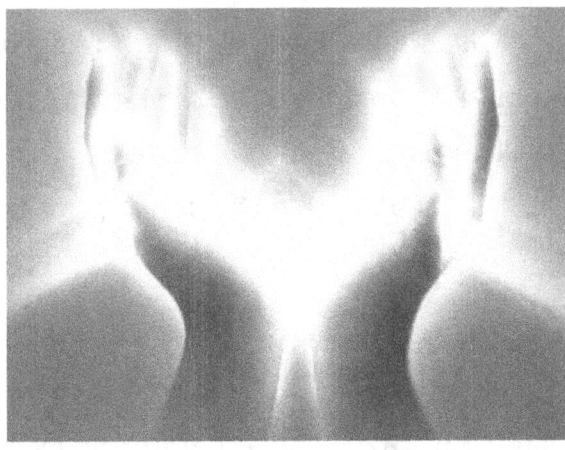

It is very easy to go down a path like this. Our society has taught us to sit down, be quiet and do what we are told. While we learn many lessons at the same time, we aren't necessarily living up to our true spiritual potential, which knows no limits and is not bound by societal law.

We must learn to live somewhat within the framework we are given, yet creating our own path that will make us truly happy. To be more specific, the basic framework would read something like, respect others, don't hurt anyone and pay your taxes. The rest is really up to you. That's pretty lenient, giving your spirit free reign over everything else. And yet most of us don't. We never reach our full potential because we are stuck living in a world of rules. As good kids, we don't want to upset anyone by doing our own thing.

Having a damaged spirit affects everything you do. For example, perhaps you have just ended a bad relationship. This could be a friend, spouse or even co-worker. This person may have taken advantage of you, asking for favors with no reciprocation, being mentally manipulative, you name it. The result is a body and mind that are disconnected from the spirit. That is, if your spirit had anything to say about it, this relationship would have ended ages ago.

The result is a general lack of life. You may have been depressed, anxious, forgoing your own needs for someone else's. Over time, the stress of this can have physical effects, leading to health problems like chronic colds and flu from a weak immune system. You could feel generally lethargic, as your body is just not energized. You may even have serious ailments like heart disease or autoimmune diseases as stress is generally considered the source of it all.

Now that this situation has resolved, whether, by your will or theirs, it is time to get your connection back. There are many resources available that we can use to get reacquainted with our inner self, and it is certainly worth working on. Once you can get back in touch with your inner self, your life comes back. On the right path, you will feel energized, motivated, and capable. Your health can improve as you will be making better choices regarding your health. You will no longer need food, alcohol, cigarettes or your crutch of choice to deal with stress.

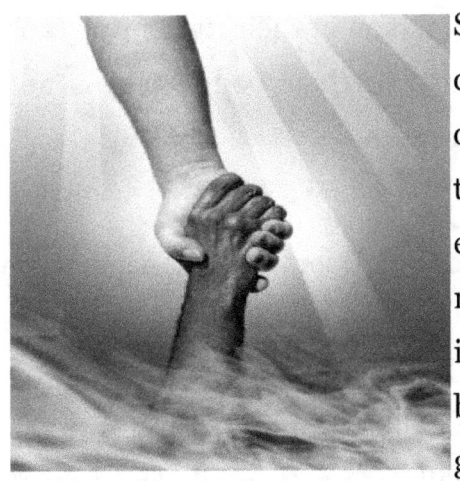

Spiritual healing comes in many different forms. There are plenty of professional healers out there that can help transform your energy and help get you on the right track. If you feel you have no idea where to start, it could be beneficial to meet with a healer to get your bearings and figure out where to go from here. With their help, you can balance your inner energy, get those energy systems aligned and flowing properly. Their guidance can give you the reassurance you need to move forward with your life and get back to normal.

If you feel more confident in your own skills, try doing some things on yourself at home. Learning practices like Reiki and meditation can be easy and very beneficial to do on your own. Many people feel more comfortable taking this journey alone, without involving someone else in their process. This is a personal choice, and as this is their wish, will likely be very successful taking solitary measures.

Do not count spiritual healing out if you feel your only problems are physical. For example, if you feel you have developed diabetes or high blood pressure out of the blue, there is a lot of work to do. Sure, you don't exercise and your diet has been poor lately, but spiritual healing can get at the root of why you have made those bad decisions in the first place. No person in their right mind (and spirit) would choose to cause harm to their bodies, stress and other issues in life are usually the reason.

While you should still see a medical doctor to manage these problems, getting reconnected with your spirit, changing things you are unhappy with in your life and getting back on your spiritual path will change all of that. Just think, if everything was going right at work, you had a wealth of great family and friends and you were generally content, wouldn't it be easier to eat better and exercise? The stress of bad relationships and situations sets off a chain reaction of negativity that leads to physical symptoms of stress.

Spiritual healing is free. It is easy, and it is what your body wants. It knows it should be deeply connected with the spirit, but our minds trick us into thinking we have it all figured out on our own. All you need to do is start listening to the very loud, very obvious signs that our spiritual self is giving us. All of the stress we feel, the ailments we develop and the gut feelings we ignore are our spirit trying to tell us we have strayed from our path. They are ways of telling us so that we may find a way back to the right path.

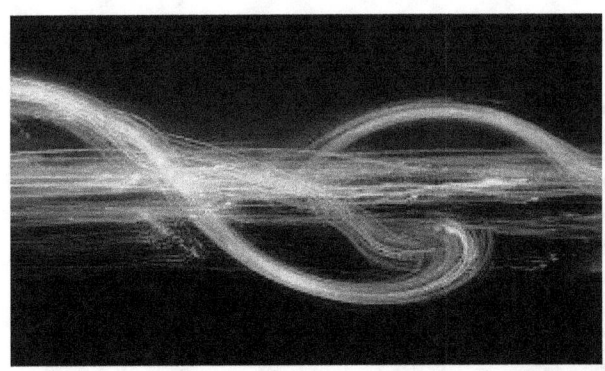

When we do get back on track and stop fighting against the energy of the universe, everything falls into place. If you feel that you just can't get anything right, it is your spirit getting louder and louder, telling you that it is time to stop whatever you are doing and change your course. This could be as simple as being a more compassionate person, letting others go first in a traffic jam, being nicer to co-workers, or even uprooting your whole life and starting over. Let things go, reduce your aggravation and let in some positivity. How about start with the road rage and figure it out from there. Bringing in positive energy instead of negativity will feed your spirit and transform your entire life. It all starts with one small move.

CHAPTER 3
Power Of Spiritual Healing

Once you find an avenue of spiritual healing, the work can begin. This can be a long road, with twists and turns. You may not know exactly where you are going, but you need to trust your intuitions and understand that your spirit is genuinely connected with the universal spirit. Energy is very simple, flowing through the path of least resistance. It knows where it is going and it can see the fastest way to get there. Your energy is just the same. Listen to it, follow it and you will end up exactly where you are supposed to be. That end just may surprise you.

If you aren't quite sure about this whole process yet, take a lesson from a few people who take steps every day to connect with their inner self and find guidance. Many have come before you, got acquainted with their inner selves, and are living better lives for it. Remember that the only end point is our final passing, and so we must continue to listen. It is never too late to start on your path to wellness, and a better quality of life.

Take Amy, for an example. Amy is the daughter of a profitable business owner and grew up working in her father's restaurant. As the business grew, it became a family joke that Amy would eventually take over the business when her father retired. At the time this was brought up, at the ripe old age of seventeen, it made

Amy grimace. The thought made her uncomfortable, but she wasn't sure why. She liked waiting tables at the restaurant with her sisters and cousins.

When college rolled around, Amy decided she would take some business management courses, in hopes of finding some motivation for taking over the restaurant. When she graduated, her father hired her on to manage the restaurant, as he stepped down to retire. It was always his dream to retire early and live off the profits from his successful venture. Amy wanted this for him as well.

Years pass, and Amy marries and has a few children. Her time is spent mostly at the restaurant, doing the books, ordering supplies and doing her best to manage. Over the years she has gained weight, eating the diner-style fare that surrounded her, doing little to move the wonderful body this universe put together for her. She becomes grouchy and unapproachable, as she is tired and overworked. Her staff turnover increases, as waiters and cooks find it hard to deal with her attitude. She gets divorced, as the relationship with her husband suffered many years of strained silence.

Amy is at a turning point. She is now middle aged, wondering what happened with her life. Her mind fills with thoughts of things she could have done to be happier, be thinner, to have maintained her marriage. All worthless thoughts, as the past is gone and cannot be changed.

As the kids stay with dad on weekends, Amy is confronted with some free time. She begins to really think, to listen. She begins to be drawn to articles online about stress management and relaxation. She eventually comes across one that peaks her interest in particular, about spiritual healing. The idea of meditation and listening to her inner self is very intriguing, likely something her spirit wanted her to see.

She begins making time to meditate on a daily basis. She starts out slow, with just a few mindful thoughts every day, and a bit of journaling her emotions. As she begins to feel her stress melt away, she explores other options, even going to a professional healer for help and guidance. She begins to notice how defeated she feels as soon as she enters the restaurant. Her spirit feels physically depleted just thinking about it.

She listens to these signs and eventually comes to the decision that she needs to get out of the business. There is no big revelation, no fireworks going off as she comes to this realization. In fact, she has no idea what she would do instead, just that managing the business is not working anymore. She is scared, anxious, and unsure what to do with this realization.

Over time, she gathers the strength to speak with her father about stepping aside. He agrees, reluctantly, but understanding that being there is slowly killing her, both physically and mentally.

Amy's spiritual healing continues with regular meditation and mindfulness. While she is drawn to many things, she always enjoyed the marketing side of the restaurant business. She always enjoyed making the flyers for weekly specials and managing an online presence. This was a creative outlet for her, and her savvy marketing skills kept the business healthy for years.

She is now pursuing a degree in marketing, building better relationships with her kids and living a more meaningful life. She has started exercising after feeling her body decline, recognizing it is an unhealthy vessel for the blossoming spirit inside.

Amy is still a work in progress but by giving in to the natural flow of her spirit, she has been able to get back to her intended path. Sure, she never expected to be a middle aged, divorced mother in college, but she is happier than she ever was at the restaurant, and her newfound motivation for life is more than enough to get her to the next adventure.

Amy's experience is not out of the ordinary, yet it is her own. We all hear about miracle success stories about how people on the brink of disaster turn it around and become millionaires. Sure, your spirit may get you there, but your spirit also isn't concerned with money. The sooner you realize that the better. Our spiritual successes are measured in happiness, contentment, love, and energy, not money.

Be open minded to this process and take money out of the equation. Many have died after living wealthy, miserable lives. They now have nothing to show for it but  their misery. Money means nothing. Discard that thought, follow your true passions, and the universe will figure out how to sustain you. Not rich, sustaining. If your passion happens to make you rich beyond your wildest dreams, you will be an exception to the rule. But if nothing else, you will be happy.

CHAPTER 4
The Third Eye

If our spirit is just energy, how can it possibly know what our true path is? How can we trust that it has our best interests in mind and that we will be led in the right direction? The idea of the spiritual 'third eye' is not a new idea. In fact, it actually comes up in some way, shape or form in just about every cultural history and religion.

Across cultures, the symbol of the pine cone denotes the third eye. Looking at the top of a pinecone, you will notice, it's symmetrical and a spiral pattern. It is seen in many pieces of art throughout the histories of many different cultures. It is often found in Hindu art, Egyptian renderings of their Gods, and even half way across the world in Mexico. Even the Pope's staff is topped with a pinecone. This symbol, the third eye shows that these Gods and higher beings held the connection to the universe, and that is why they were wise and powerful above the rest.

Also asymmetrical is its physical manifestation in the brain. The pineal gland is science's answer for the third eye. The pineal gland is found dead center in the brain. It is thought to be responsible for the production of melatonin, a hormone that helps regulate our sleep cycles, but the rest is unknown. While new studies are few and far between, there are links to a chemical called dimethyltryptamine (DMT) that is thought to bring on vivid dreams and visuals.

While many synthetic hallucinogenic drugs try to mimic this chemical, it is made naturally in most mammals and is usually only used during the REM cycle of sleep, and under times of great stress. It is thought that the phenomenon of your life flashing before your eyes in a life-threatening situation is actually caused by this chemical. Pretty interesting.

For spiritual followers, the pineal gland does what it has always done, and that is to be the gland responsible for connecting the body to the spirit. Many cultures believe that this gland, or the third eye, has the ability to see things for what they truly are, to see above and beyond the short-sightedness of our lives and look at the bigger picture.

Without thinking about a specific gland, consider how harnessing the power of your third eye can change your life. Without proving that it actually exists scientifically, we still know it is there. We use it to some degree in everyday life. It is that guiding force that gives us gut feelings about bad situations. It helps you make good decisions.

Unfortunately, it is possible to ignore the wisdom of our third eye. While we may not realize we are even doing it, our brains push aside the all-seeing power of the third eye and decide to take the road that seems easier, seems like a better idea. In reality, following the guidance of your third eye may make for a messier road, but the outcome will be much greater. Without having the ability to see above what you are currently entrenched in, you could be tempted to take what seems like the right way out. Your third eye can see above the mess and can guide you out properly, but only if you follow the signs it gives you.

The third eye illuminates and sees the wisdom of the universe, and it is useful to have that on your side. Each and every one of us has that power within us, yet most of us do end up ignoring it. We often do things for the wrong reasons. For example, taking a job that you are not passionate about just to pay the bills. Sure, it puts food on the table, but remember that deep down, you are suppressing your inner spirit by not following its predetermined path.

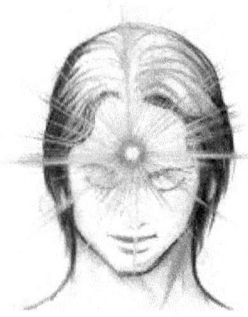

While it may seem like a noble cause to sacrifice your happiness for the sake of your family, to make this a long-term plan just won't work out for your third eye. Remember that your inner self is pure energy. It does not care about money or social status, it cares that it is fulfilling its universal connection. Going against its wishes means that you are going against the flow of energy, something that will fail you in the long run. While it may seem easier to buckle down and make money where you are, looking ahead, you will have been better off taking steps toward your inner destiny.

Your inner self can see what is ahead, and for our brains, they make sense of this by calling it psychic ability. Some people are able to know what is going to happen before it happens. For most people, this is unexplainable, and therefore must be a trick. While the true cause is still a scientific mystery, those with this gift are likely just more tuned into their third eye.

While it may just feel like intuition to some, others may literally be able to see the future. It compares to different levels of blindness. Some people can see 20/20, every inch of any object, while others can only recognize shadows and light. Those who are blind compare to those with only simple intuition while the person with 20/20 can see the future.

Their brains are much more connected with the universe, giving their third eye the ability to see into the futures of others as well. They can see and sense the energy and can make sense of which way it will go, which plays out in real-life situations.

No matter your preferred understanding of your third eye, it is imperative that we listen to it constantly. The third eye is with us to guide us on our life journey. Instead of working against it, trust that it knows the way and just follow it. While it may seem like you are headed down the wrong path sometimes, if it feels right in your gut, it is probably your third eye reassuring you that you are on the right track.

CHAPTER 5
Finding Happiness Through Your Spirit

Our ultimate happiness can be found when we follow the wishes of our inner spirit. It is very easy to get down on ourselves and be beaten down by life. Plenty of bad things happen and things don't go as we expect. Many people say that it is necessary to go through some bad things to learn important lessons, and to appreciate when things go right.

If you are a believer in spiritual destiny, like many do, this is right up your alley. We have to trust that our spirit knows exactly where we will end up, and as long as we trust our intuitions and believe that we will get there, we have nothing to worry about. It is much easier to understand and accept losses and setbacks when we believe that it is something we need to get through before we reach our true destiny.

Having this divine knowledge makes it so much easier to be happy. If you are truly connected with your spirit, following your path, energy will flow through you like you would not believe. You will have the capacity to do anything you set your mind to do, and things will seem to fall into place all on their own.

Many people have no belief in this so-called spiritual wisdom, but the truth is, they just call it something else. Think about all of those people who find success through hard work. They say they put their nose to the grindstone and things turned out the way they did because of sweat and hard work.

No spiritual destiny ever came true without a little hard work. Happiness and destiny are met only when you are all-in on something. The only thing your spirit does is give you the energy to get through all that you must endure to get to where you are going. It is that drive and stamina that give those on their true path the ability to follow through and reach their goals. Those who give up on a goal do not do so because they are quitters. They are just on the wrong path.

There is no shame in giving up on a goal if you no longer believe in your heart that it is your destiny. Remember that our inner spirit may put us through things to teach us a lesson that will serve us down the road. It will be necessary to correct your course from time to time.

What will be your guide is your overall happiness. If you are following your dreams and working hard, you will feel good and you will be happier than you have ever been. No, not every day, there will still be some duds sprinkled in, but overall, you will feel motivated and willing to continue forward progress.

It is possible that you have not experienced true happiness in a long time. Children are often able to be in touch with their inner selves much more than adults. They have not yet been jaded by the world and can feel that sense of connection. In your adult life, you may have had the illusion of happiness, but have not felt it in quite a while.

That is fine, everyone needs a starting point. The goal is to make positive progress toward being happier. By indulging your spirit and giving in to being silly, taking time for yourself and just enjoying the moment, your spirit can become a little stronger, a little brighter. Keep following that feeling as your guide to your true path, and your ultimate happiness.

The idea of happiness is somewhat intangible. We all know what it feels like to be giddy, like a kid in a candy store. Maybe riding roller coasters or some other hobbies give you that feeling of freedom, of joy. We need to find and

incorporate more moments like that in our everyday lives. For too long, we have built our days around doing things that we are 'required' to do, instead of sprinkling it in. Instead, we should build our days around doing things we love, and want to do, sprinkling in some of the administrative duties, like dishes and making money.

While you may scoff at this alternate idea of reality, it can, and does, exist. There are people out there right now that absolutely love what they do every day. Maybe it is something that seems boring to you, like being an accountant or lawyer, but if that is their true calling, they wake up every day ready to get started. Their natural energy just flows, and they make the most of every moment, at the end of the day feeling happy and fulfilled after carrying out their universal task.

At this point, there is a good chance that you are feeling overwhelmed. The idea of changing your life around to include more happiness may seem unrealistic and unfathomable. Let's try to consider what your third eye might be seeing right now. Maybe your destiny is to become a world traveling philanthropist with every country checked off your passport list. Your third eye can see all of the event leading up to this, like memories, and knows everything that came before that end goal was worth it.

Think about a major milestone in your life. Perhaps you graduated college and landed a great job that is satisfying and happens to pay the bills. When those happy moments occur, it is easy to look back and say that a headache and turmoil of college was well worth the trouble. Your third eye does this constantly, like a dog running ahead of its master, then running back to urge them forward.

Your inner self is like a good friend saying to you, "Look, I know the way, just follow me and I will get you there safe and sound." All you need to do is trust it. Give in and trust that your inner self, the ultimate extension of you, has all of the answers. Stop outsmarting your inner spirit with your knowledge in the moment. Tapping into your intuition and following those moments of clarity and wisdom will get you where you need to go.

CHAPTER 6

Lifting The Spirit With Prayer

Before you skip this chapter, give it a chance. Many people nowadays prefer not to participate in a formal religion, but many still do. As we discussed before, many religions pray to a God that is simply a higher being. It is all-knowing and a force of love. All religion has done is put a different name on the universal energy that connects us all. That being said, praying to said energy does not need to be religious.

For some, even the word 'prayer' gives them a lurching feeling, as they associate it with religion. Many view the idea of religion as an unsavory practice, not seeing the original intent of the practice and that is fine. Everyone will connect with the universal spirit in their own, unique way, that is the nature of our different energies.

So, to include everyone in a non-religious way, instead of calling it 'prayer', let's call it connection. That is what praying is all about, after all. People talk with God about their problems and struggles, praying that God gives the wisdom and strength to make it through.

The spirit can be healed through prayer. As we imagine that our inner self is made up of a spark of energy, it is easy to see how this would work. Think about how energy works. At its most basic, it is made up of positive and negative particles. They are generally attracted to each other, and they exist only to find and pair with each other. That's it. These particles will move heaven and earth to be together, and so they travel the path of least resistance to reach each other.

It would only make sense, then, that when your life has taken a downturn, and negativity starts to creep in, that asking for help from the positivity of the universe would even you out. If this was completely true, everyone would be balanced, and the universe would be in total harmony. In reality, our individual spirits have mechanisms to protect themselves. Our bodies house our spirits and protect them from harm.

If our bodies and minds do not let negativity in, our spirits will be unaffected. If they do, it will unbalance our spirit and suck energy from our very cores. As an example, think about a real-life scenario we have all likely experienced. We all know that one person that is always negative. Maybe they are a co-worker or acquaintance. No matter who it is, this person always has something bad to say or is complaining about something. Nothing in their world ever goes right and they insist on talking about it.

First and foremost, this person is reaching out for help in their own, very annoying way. Their life is off track and they have no idea where to start fixing it, and so they complain. Second, it is not your responsibility to fix them, the universe will take care of it eventually. It *is* your job to protect yourself from the negativity that you are faced with. While it may seem easy to commiserate with that person, take the high road and try and perk them up without getting engrossed in the mess.

When negativity inevitably sets in, there are ways to counteract it by asking for help from the universe. A simple conversation with the energy of the universe can help draw some positivity to you. The fact that you are willing to have this connection assumes that your mind and spirit are open to it, and that is a big factor. Your mind can be guarded, and although asking for help, may not be ready to receive it.

Keep your mind open and let it all out. You may choose to have an internal conversation, or if you are suffering quite severely, have an open, out-loud dialogue. The universe is your therapist. Tell it about the awful time you are having at your job, or how you are regretting moving to a new home. Don't be afraid to ask for specific things, just know how to do it.

When asking the universe for something, you must understand that you may not get it. Like a kid asking Santa for a new bike, you may in fact, not get that new sports car you've been longing for. The universe knows your path and what is best for you, therefore sending you things that *you* think you need isn't always in the cards.

A more reasonable request would be to ask for the guidance necessary to make the right moves when the time is right. Take the example of moving to a new city and 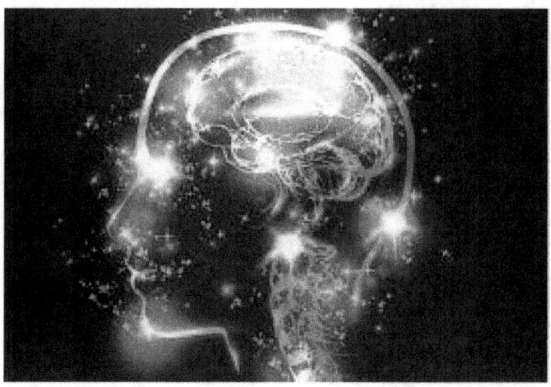 starting a new job. Maybe you were very excited at first, ready for the change. Now that you are here, the job isn't what you thought it would be, and the apartment you rented is less than ideal.

You teeter back and forth about staying or going, and you are really at a loss for what to do. Asking the universe for help is perfectly reasonable. After you have asked, you're responsible for looking out for the signals it leaves to help you make the decision. It could be as simple as making a new friend that helps you get acquainted with the city. Or perhaps something as loud as the company you work for closing its doors (even though they just hired you!). Sometimes the messages are clear, literally closing a door to open a window. Others are more subtle, like starting a friendship.

There are many ways to pray or connect with the universe, and it is up to you to decide what works best for you. Maybe you take up meditation to reconnect with the universe. Concentrating your thoughts and using guided imagery during meditation can be just as effective as having that conversation. Center your efforts on imagining the things you want out of life.

Try not to be selfish and focused on one thing, but pan out to the overall picture. Imagine yourself on a big front porch on a summer day, birds chirping and kids laughing. The feeling and energy of that moment is something the universe can recognize, which is better than asking for a big house in the suburbs. If these ideas interest you, be sure to read Chapter 7, which is more concentrated on guided imagery and meditation.

Even if you aren't asking for something specific, you will likely always be asking for something positive. With that, your spirit will be able to accept some positive energy from the universe, strengthening you from the inside out.

CHAPTER 7
Visualization And Guided Imagery

Guided imagery is a nifty technique used during meditation, and is great for reducing stress, and is a tool for connecting with the universal energy. Guided imagery can be done individually or with the help of a therapist or other health professional. Therapeutically speaking, it is good for a number of things including breaking bad habits, facing fears and relaxing an anxious mind.

The idea behind this novel technique is very basic. The mind is a quick, tactful organ that can easily outthink our spiritual guidance. It has increased in size through evolution, allowing us to make individual decisions, somewhat to the dismay of the universal energy. When left to our own devices, our decisions can be short-sighted and selfish.

The brain also gets overwhelmed fairly easily. Think about the last little bad thing that happened to you. For example, you spill coffee on your new shirt in the car on the way to work. Yes, it was a little hot, but not life-threatening in any way. Your relaxed and laid-back spirit recognizes this as a small, insignificant hiccup in the grand scheme of things.

Your brain, on the other hand, has already spiraled out of control. This new stain on your shirt means you will not look professional at your presentation today. It won't go well, you will not get that promotion at work. The house you want to buy is now way out of reach because you cannot afford it without the promotion. Your kids will not go to the good school, setting them back and damaging them. No ivy league school and they will end up doing mindless jobs, just like you. Wow, that was exhausting, and all from a small coffee stain.

Stress and anxiety are just common place these days, and so we must find tactics for sidestepping these downward mind spirals and get back to the reality of the situation. That is, everything will turn out just how it is supposed to, so worrying about a coffee stain is a complete waste of time.

Guided imagery can be used as a technique to reduce this stress and anxiety in the moment. Instead of the coffee stain derailing your day (and your life, apparently), try some guided imagery instead. As you drive, imagine how you want this meeting to go. You walk in, confident and tall, ready to go. As you begin the presentation, you make a clever joke about the stain on your shirt and move on. Everybody chuckles. You deliver your presentation, which amazes everyone, and your promotion is now secure.

Not only does this technique lower your anxiety and increase your confidence, it is affirming positive things and collecting positive energy from the universe. With it, you can now move forward and make that daydream a reality.

Anytime we hold on to stress and anxiety, we shut our spirits down, refusing helpful energy from outside. By breaking down that wall and letting some positive thoughts flow through, we can reconnect with the universal energy and draw more positivity towards us. With that, we can do all of the things we dreamed of doing.

Guided imagery can be a powerful tool, we just need to know how to activate it. If you are unfamiliar with guided imagery, it may be beneficial to meet with a professional to help you get started, although you can  certainly do it on your own. A professional can help you build images and show you how to guide your mind to these images when they are needed most. Soundtracks with pre-recorded imagery sessions can help you do this in the privacy of your own home.

If you are confident that you are mentally acute enough to guide the image yourself, go for it. It can be difficult to do on your own, as your mind will have a tendency to wander back to its place among the chaos. If you can stay focused on your image, exploring every sense of it, you will be successful, and it is definitely worth giving it a try before getting help.

A session may begin much like meditation. The goal is to relax you and keep your mind from racing. To allow your imagination to take over, close your eyes. Your prompter will then ask you to imagine a specific scene, like a sunny meadow. They will use minute details, asking you to focus on each and every one. You will imagine how the wind feels on your skin, the sun on your face, the color of the tall, golden grass, and the sound of crickets and birds all around you.

It may help to use a physical image, like a picture, to guide you at first. While you can only see the image in a picture, it can help prompt what it might feel like to be in that scene. The smells, feelings, temperature, can all be imagined with a little practice.

The idea is to focus your mind on something other than what is currently going on, and that is why it works so well with stress. By guiding the scene using all of your senses, the brain becomes preoccupied on this new, happy, relaxed thought, instead of on whatever chaos you are currently involved in. It has the power to remove you from a stressful situation, if only in your mind. Once you have gone through a session or two with a professional, it could be a great tool to use on your own.

Reducing stress through guided imagery has many health benefits. Stress is considered the root of all disease in the body. When stress hormones are activated, it causes many changes and shifts throughout, causing things like high blood pressure, heart disease, a less effective immune system, and much more. Acutely, stress causes headaches and decreased attention span, something we could all live without.

It is impossible to rid yourself of stress completely, but using techniques like guided imagery to better manage it can improve the quality of your life and strengthen the connection you seek with the universal power. This energy can heal you from the inside out, so why not try and draw more of it toward you?

CHAPTER 8

Radionics, Using Waves Of Energy As Healing

The concept of Radionics goes right along with everything we have been talking about. The idea that the electromagnetic waves put out by the body can be used to diagnose problems is right up our alley.

The goal with radionics therapy is to pinpoint disturbances in energy that can be causing health issues or overall discontent. While this idea may seem a little futuristic, the theories of this energy healing go back to early civilizations. Many Eastern cultures believe that the energy field of the body is made up of seven chakras that align themselves along the axis of the body.

The energy is meant to flow through them, and when in proper order, delivers nourishing energy to every inch of the body. If one of those chakras is blocked, entire parts of the body may not be receiving the energy it needs to function optimally, therefore causing problems. Radionics simply takes this idea and finds a way to tangibly see where the energy is off.

The practice was originally created by Dr. Albert Abrams in the late eighteen hundreds. Since then, several other doctors have adopted the practice, evolving it into what it is today. His idea is that every living thing is surrounded by an energy field, and we can use technology to 'see' the energy field and find its weak spots. The technology works much like a temperature monitor in the dark. You can see the energy given off by a person, and when you see cooler, darker spots, it is obvious that energy is not reaching that area.

The best way to describe radionics is by comparing it to dousing. This old practice used forks to locate water sources in the ground. Experienced dowsers could walk across a piece of property, forks in hand, and be able to find water just by reading the forks. The metals in these instruments react to the energy field surrounding the water, like magnets attracting each other. This practice was very common before modern technology made it possible to see water underground for the purpose of digging wells.

If this fool-proof practice could find water deep in the ground, why is it so impossible to believe that we can also study the energy fields that surround each and every one of us? Although we cannot see it, energy exists all around us, and it affects every single thing we do. It cannot be ignored, and alternative ideas like this should be used in combination with modern medicine to really get a full picture of what is going on in and around the body.

This practice is not meant to diagnose any disease, only to see the possible causes related to energy. Thinking very basically about disease, it is simply an interruption in normalcy in whatever region of the body it is affecting. Chronic kidney failure is caused by a problem in the kidneys. In terms of energy, the body is not able to provide the energy the kidneys need to function correctly, and/or rid itself of infection or cancer that may be affecting the area.

That being said, the concept of radionics also takes into consideration the idea of healing. If we can find sources of energy instability, we should be able to fix it by adding energy into the area from the universe, and correcting chakras when necessary.

Many holistic therapies, like Reiki center around this idea that we can concentrate energy on spots where it is needed most to induce healing. The interesting thing about radionics is the claim that healing can occur from a distance, unlike more familiar practices like Reiki. Practitioners can take a drop of blood or a lock of hair, perform energy healing on it from a distance, and the body feels the results.

By now, you may be thinking that this is a little far out for you, or perhaps, you have seen this work and understand it. The Radionics Associated backs up the idea that most practitioners first scoffed at this idea, calling it mostly nonsense. The truth is, they aren't really sure why it works, yet it does.

If you are interested in this therapy, you must find a professional that is trained to read the radionics instruments and determine a proper diagnosis for you.  This should be relatively simple, as practitioners from halfway across the world can do this for you, and you never need to leave the comfort of your own home. You send them something of yours, whether the lock of hair or even a photo.

A carefully planned phone session will follow, in which the practitioner asks a multitude of questions regarding each and every system in your body. While speaking with you, the instrument is focused on the item you have sent and reads it. The professional will be able to decipher any energy changes that occur with certain questions and help make a diagnosis. This is meant to work alongside modern medicine to help diagnose the energy problem behind your ailment, so that work may be done to heal it. The same practitioner claims to be able to send needed energy through the object to heal you from afar.

Scientifically speaking, there is no evidence to support or refute these claims, but anecdotal evidence is overwhelmingly positive. Why not give it a try?

CHAPTER 9
Bodhicitta

Unless you have been engrossed in the field of alternative medicine for some time, you have probably never heard of Bodhicitta. It would be surprising if you actually knew the definition of this term, as it is very vague and ethereal in nature. To sum it up, it is the energy of loving and kindness that you have for the earth, the people around you, and every other living thing.

We have all heard that we need to be kind to others, and treat them as you would wish to be treated. While this is a good concept to live by, we often shape our actions around this idea, but not our thoughts. Think about the last time you dealt with a difficult person, specifically a customer or client. It is literally your job to be nice and help people, yet, you only do so because you are told. The idea of Bodhicitta means that you genuinely care for people, want to help, and you can feel compassion and love for them.

Most of us are severely lacking in Bodhicitta, only feeling this way toward a select few people in our lives, and that love is not usually unconditional. The sad thing is, if we were to open up to others in this way, our lives would be exponentially better. Bodhicitta, when achieved, is a source of pure positive energy and light, just what our spirit needs to heal and grow. In turn, our quality of life will improve, we will see the world in a different way, and even our health ailments can resolve as a result of all of the extra energy.

For those of you who pray, or have recently decided to get reconnected with your inner spirit and the universal energy, you should know that you need Bodhicitta for it to work. You need to carry an open mind and ask for things that are unselfish and really have no ulterior motives. The same thing goes with meditation. If the only reason you do it is that you think your monetary success will improve in the end, it will not work. You must be willing to do things for the sole purpose of getting reconnected, and the rest will work from there.

Achieving Bodhicitta requires a complete, sincere attitude change, and this isn't something that happens overnight. Instead, we can make small steps every day by reforming how we think about things and see other people. We can start by turning our pessimistic, judging thoughts into ones that see the other side of the equation. For example, you may not see eye to eye with someone. This happens all the time. Instead of avoiding them and casting them off as someone you prefer not to associate with, take the time to see things from their point of view.

This person is innately good, just as every spirit is. They may have lost their way and are going through some things you cannot even imagine. It may have made them mean, selfish or inconsiderate of others. Instead of getting angry, which is easy, try taking a step back and consider what they may have going on. Feel compassion for their situation, find common ground to relate to.

Don't worry about how this person is affecting you it is selfish. Instead, wonder how you are affecting them, and find ways to help them. Bodhicitta is the absence of selfishness, and an abundance of will to love others. It is with this that we have the best quality of life.

Think about your sources of guilt. Many of us would say that their biggest regrets were related to how we interacted with someone else. Maybe we regret not finishing college, but what weighs more heavily on the mind is arguments with people, and feeling as if you have done someone wrong. The guilt leads to anxiety and completely throws off our energy field.

While it may not be possible to make amends with every person you have wronged in the past, it is possible to move forward with a new attitude, one which is respectful and loving of others. Go about each and every moment with gratitude and appreciation toward others. If you aren't sure if you have reached Bodhicitta, don't worry, the universe will let you know.

To reach a more enlightened state, go about your life with a different attitude. Challenge yourself to be more compassionate, accepting and loving toward others, even complete strangers. No, this will not happen overnight, but imagine that every little step in that direction illuminating more and more of your inner spirit.

CHAPTER 10

Channeling

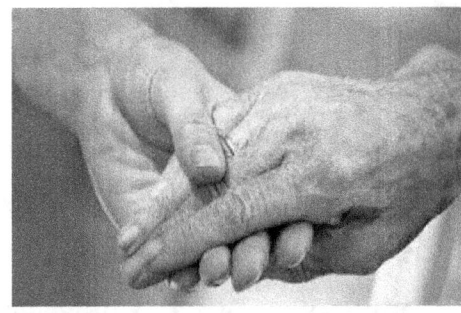

We have discussed several ways to connect with the energy system of the universe, and channeling is no different. This concept takes stock in the concept of receiving wisdom from a higher power. We talked a lot about tapping into the wisdom of your inner spirit, and channeling helps us connect with the universe as a whole, and even specific beings.

The purpose of channeling is to find truth and wisdom from a divine, all-knowing source: the universe. We must also learn from living things around us how to live our best lives in harmony. Since this is such an intangible thing for our minds to wrap around, let us begin with an example.

The most popular, television-worthy form of channeling is through a medium. This person is extra perceptive to energy in the universe and has the ability to connect with energies on different spiritual planes, mainly, the spirits of those who have departed this planet. As energy can neither be created or destroyed, only moved, it is easy to imagine that our spirits simply travel somewhere else when we leave this earth. The spirit is still there and can make contact with our world.

Mediums channel these spirits through their mind by reading energies and picking up on small signals from other beings. Channeling works in the same way and actually, reads much like the process of praying. In the end, the real goal is to accept the wisdom and knowledge of wiser beings, whether spirits that came before or of the earth itself.

Many people consider the idea of channeling past spirits is a bad idea. Creating a connection to negative spirits full of revenge and malice via Ouija boards is the basis for many horror movies, and it never ends well. For the most part, the universe is full of positivity, and unless you allow negativity to flow, connecting with spirits on another plane is harmless.

To sense this idea a little better, think of channeling as plugging yourself into the energy system like you would plug in a lamp in your wall. On your television, pure energy signals are transformed into lights, images, and colors, as well as sound. All of this information travels through cable, which is an astounding idea in itself, so why wouldn't we be able to receive messages from other planes through universal energy?

You do not need to be a true medium to channel energy, you simply need to be open and willing to it. Again, this goes back to simply asking the universe for enlightenment and answers to the questions you seek to know. By channeling our inner selves in the universe, we can reconnect and gain knowledge by its presence. The goal is to find love, acceptance, and power through this spirit, so that we may carry that out in our daily lives.

While some channeling does occur during meditation, it isn't necessary to actively meditate to do it. In fact, channeling is a natural thing and requires no specific environment to do it. However, quiet, restful environments in which you can relax help prime your mind for accepting energy and channeling your inner self.

Practicing yoga, mindful meditation, Reiki or Tai Chi are great, relaxing ways to stretch your body, align your chakras and open your mind to the idea of channeling. There are two main types of channeling; passive and active. Doing activities like described and letting your mind wander is passive channeling. Your mind is open and ready to receive whatever information the universe decides to send you.

Active channeling can be great if you are really in desperate need of guidance. In a state such as this, it will be very difficult to passively channel, as your mind is stressed and focused on something in particular. Put that energy to good  use and push it out into the atmosphere. Send your thought waves out and see what you get in response. This would be like sending a radio signal into space and waiting for extraterrestrial life to say something back.

While we may need to wait awhile for aliens, the universal energy response is pretty immediate. If you send out a question, and your energy is urgent, the universe will send you back the energy and wisdom you need to balance yourself out. You do not need to wait in line, as energy just flows where it is needed.

We must also not forget about channeling between living beings here on this earth. If you have ever had a pet, you have participated in channeling. We can often speak with dogs and cats, just by eye contact alone. We can sense what they are feeling, and vice versa. The ability to love an animal unconditionally is much easier than loving a human in that way. For some reason, we are much more guarded about human contact than we are with animals. This unyielding love opens the door to Bodhicitta and creates a perfect energy exchange.

Once this is established, whether, through animal or human contact, information and energy can be shared across the energy field. As if one small step away from reading their mind, you are able to understand, feel compassion for, and love that living being. You can heal what ails them with your love and energy, and you can accept love and energy in return in perfect balance.

We can see the truth of this with the adoption of pets. Many people who have lost loved ones often adopt pets. The goal is to keep them company, but really, these animals have Bodhicitta, as they are  more in-touch and enlightened by the universal spirit. They are able to send us energy and heal us, and by returning this favor, we create a lasting bond with animals that cannot be broken.

Channeling is an amazing, process that can heal your inner spirit. Start by putting your signals out into the universe, and see what comes back. Connect with the living things around you as well. It is so easy to get caught up in our own problems that we forget to take a time to connect with our spouses, children, pets and even strangers. The more connected you can become with the creatures that share this energy field with you, the better off you will be.

CHAPTER 11
Color Healing

How is it possible that looking at certain colors can heal you? The answer is very simple: color is simply the visual representation of energy as light. Rays from the sun are just energy and elicit light and color in the right environments. It relates directly, then to all of the work we have done with energy healing thus far.

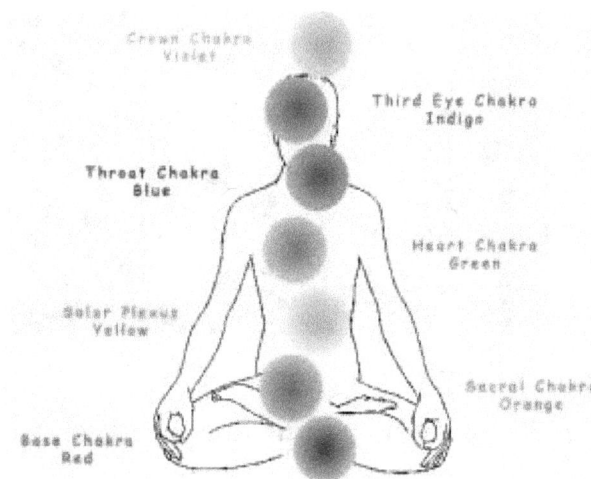

If we can emit certain energy through color alone, we can repair our chakras and focus this energy where it will do the most good. Each color is correlated to each of the seven chakras. Red is associated with the root chakra, located at the base of our tailbone, and is what keeps us grounded. It also gives sensations and feelings of safety and security.

The color orange represents the sacral chakra, whose energy is concentrated just under the belly button. It gives feelings of desire and represents procreation. Yellow is for the solar plexus chakra, located just above the belly button in the upper abdomen. This chakra is all about the heart and gives us the ability to love and have compassion for each other. Notably, without alignment of this chakra, we have no hope of reaching Bodhicitta.

Blue represents the throat chakra, which gives us the energy to speak clearly and concisely for optimal communication with others. Indigo represents the mysticism behind the third eye, centered in the middle of our foreheads. This color is considered so mystical because of the intangible yet noticeable power of our inner wisdom. Finally, purple represents the crown chakra, the highest peak on our bodies. This is thought of as the connection point between our physical being and the universal energy. Energy enters our body through this chakra.

While color emitting lights are available on the market, there are other ways to use color therapy. Changing the colors of a room can help change the mood and feel of a space. Just as color corresponds to each chakra, it emits similar chakra feelings into room just by the color of the walls. The only problem with painting an entire room one shade of color is energy overbalance. That is, your crown chakra could be off, prompting you to paint a room purple. That quickly gets resolved and now your heart chakra is off. You would need to paint the room green.

With interior design, you are better off creating spaces that have pops of color that can easily be changed, like with colorful throw pillows or artwork of a specific shade of color. Those things can be easily changed.

If interior design isn't in the cards, try little things like bringing up pictures on your computer that are a certain color. If you are in need of some yellow, just search for images in that color and take a gander at it for a while. Make it your desktop at work so every time you open your computer, you get a little dose of light therapy.

Depending on your upset chakra, getting a total change of scenery may just do the trick as well. Sometimes when you are feeling low and need a refreshing pick me up, a trip to a different environment is just enough to realign your chakras. Say you are feeling a bit crabby and cannot relate to others. Your heart chakra may be blocked. Taking a hike through a green forest will help bring air into your lungs and energy into your heart, realigning your chakra.

Perhaps you are having problems communicating with your partner. Your existence has been nothing but arguing about miscommunications. Likely your throat chakra is out of whack. A trip to the ocean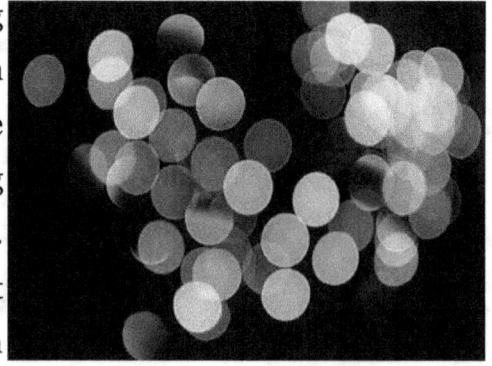

and surrounding yourself with blue sky and water should fix you right up and give you the ability to properly communicate your intentions.

Since color has so much representation of these chakras, it makes perfect sense to heal them using color therapy. Using specific light waves that transmit these colors can help realign the chakras to get them working optimally. Light is absorbed through our eyes first and foremost, but also through every inch of our skin.

Scientifically speaking, we know that our skin has the ability to absorb sunlight because of Vitamin D. This vitamin is made from cholesterol circulating in our bodies. It can be transformed into Vitamin D when a chemical reaction, set off by sunlight, occurs. The body is a big and complex place. While it has not been scientifically proven that color therapy has any specific health benefits, the results are clear. Remember that light boxes for Vitamin D activation have not been proven either, yet many doctors still recommend it based off of anecdotal evidence.

Having a meaningful experience with light therapy requires a little bit of legwork. That is, you must know what color light you will need to have the biggest effect. First and foremost, you must make a connection with whatever ails you to a correlating chakra.

When thinking about light therapy as a whole, we must consider that the chakras are connected. One must come before the next, and if one is not functioning properly, it affects all of the other ones as well. If you are serious about beginning color therapy, make sure you satisfy the needs of each chakra instead of constantly focusing on just one. This is all about balance. A little-targeted color therapy could be just what you need to invigorate your spirit and get going.

CHAPTER 12

Meditation-Methods And Benefits To Connecting To Spirit

We have touched upon the idea of meditation many times throughout this book. If you are new to the idea of meditation, this chapter is for you. Here, we will discuss the many ways to meditate, so that you may find a method that works well for you. Everyone will respond differently to different types of meditation, so you are invited to openly try each one until you find something that speaks to you.

The practice of meditation has been around for thousands of years, and across all cultures. As you do some research, you will find that every culture throughout the ages has found a way to connect with the universe, in a multitude of different ways. The practice was thought to originate in the Eastern countries near India and Nepal, with some of the greatest spiritual leaders emerging from this area.

Who is to say who began with meditation though, as it is human nature to want to connect with the universe on a higher level.

Everyone does it in some way, whether calling it proper meditation or not.

The Vedas, ancient Indians were the first to begin documenting meditation. At the same time, similar methods popped up in China and Japan in the same timeframe, over 1500 years ago. We also know that Native Americans, both in North and South America were also meditating, and connecting with the universal spirit. They used chanting and dancing and often made meditation and connection a communal event. Since then, these documented methods of meditation spread across the world, morphing into what it is today.

For the most part, modern meditation is a solitary event. We get so much interaction with others in the community, that it becomes a source of stress. We work and meet deadlines, need to pay the bills and be responsible for daily things in life. We must have moments of solitude that allow us to reconnect individually with our inner spirit and the energies of the universe. We need to plug back into this ethereal energy before we may begin renewed again.

As you carry forward in life, you may find those different methods of meditation work better for you, depending on the situation. Follow the needs of your spirit and do what works best. This does not mean that you need to meditate the same way all the time.

Our spirits are free and fleeting, and so expecting the same methods of relaxation and connection to provide us the same feelings are unreasonable.

We really need to seek answers to universal questions, which will vary day by day, even minute by minute. We each need to get connected with the spirit and our predestined purpose in order to live our best lives. Many people circle around these ideas but never fully embrace the idea of destiny. We like to believe that we are ultimately in control of how our lives turn out, and yes, this has some truth. We have control over whether or not we fulfill our destinies and lead meaningful happy lives, or whether we follow the guidance of our physical mind and circle the drain.

We get so caught up in the idea of success through tangible things like money and things. We forget that there is something much bigger. Many relate to the fact that we cannot take those physical things with us when we go, and that is true. Someday, your spirit will leave this earth and will have nothing to show for itself except for the experiences it had. Our spirit grows when it is happy and fulfilled, and money and luxury are not part of that equation.

To begin, meditation, in general, is the process of guiding your body and mind toward relaxation. On a deeper level, we are able to connect with our inner spirit. This benefits us as deeper connection with our inner selves drives our lives. This spirit is responsible for guiding us in our physical bodies. Our brains have a tendency to try and work on their own, without considering the well-being of our spirit. Through meditation, we can reconnect with the spirit and be guided on our true path.

The most popular type of meditation is passive, in which you allow energy from the universe to flow through you until an equilibrium is reached. This is easy to do if you are just beginning meditation and aren't sure where to start. The idea is to clear your mind and let it be open to whatever the universe wants to send it.

Getting your mind to this state is the purpose of meditation, and there are a couple of options to do this. Both involve finding a quiet, noise-free space in which to practice. Ideally, a bedroom or other quiet room is best, but it is not always possible to find such a space, hence why you are stressed and anxious in the first place.

The room should be comfortable in temperature, and the light dim, as to not blind the senses. Once you have found this space, it is time to get comfortable. Sitting or lying down is best, but the idea isn't to fall asleep. Most methods then ask you to focus solely on the inhale and exhale of breath. Allowing your mind to concentrate on this makes all other thoughts and feelings fall away.

For many people, focusing on breath alone is not enough to get their mind to clear. As you try to concentrate, the mind tends to wander back to thoughts and problems that consumed you moments before. Using sound therapy, like a soundtrack of soothing noises or thinking or speaking a keyword like 'calm' over and over can help maintain that focus.

This type of meditation allows your mind to sort itself out and start thinking again with a clean slate. Imagine that throughout the day, your mind takes out files to find pieces of information. Instead of putting those files neatly back, they lay strewn all over the place. Meditation allows your brain's keeper to take a break and clean up the mess, preparing you to start again.

Other types of meditation do not require so much focus. Most of the time, the mind is consumed with stress because there is just no time to think things through. During the day, we are bombarded with all sorts of requests and responsibilities. Taking a few moments to meditate and do nothing physically gives our minds time to think things through.

If you decide to meditate this way, let your thoughts stream through your mind as you sit still, with your eyes closed. Instead of getting stressed by these thoughts, let them pass through without assigning any emotion to them. For example, if you are thinking about a project deadline at work, think only about the tasks that need to get done, and not how you will feel doing them. This will give clarity to the assignment without deeming them overwhelming or stressful.

If you are just beginning with meditation, these passive methods will probably work best for you. Just as we hear that exercising every day is good for maintaining our health, daily meditation helps us maintain the health of our spirit. We may not feel stressed every day, and so we may think that meditating is not necessary every day. On the contrary, choosing to practice every day will help maintain that level of calm and collectedness so we will be better prepared for when stress does occur.

Meditation is something that you need to make time for, even if it is just a few minutes. Make it part of your daily routine by adding in small increments of time in throughout the day. Use our five-minute meditation guide in the following chapter to get started. This exercise is meant to calm the mind and bring you back to center quickly so that you may carry on with your day.

As meditation is all about relaxation, trying to incorporate it either as you wake up in the morning, or as you settle into sleep are good practices. Likely, you are already partly relaxed and can use this time to better connect with your inner spirit. Meditating as you wake can help prepare you for the day, getting off to a good start. Practicing just before bed clears the mind and helps your body prepare for sleep. Your body and mind will thank you in the morning.

We can also use active meditation to our advantage. If you are just beginning, you will likely benefit from passive meditation at first. This method gives you the ability to center your thoughts. As you get to practice with passive meditation, you can begin then actively asking the universe for what you need.

Many types of meditation call for active use of the brain. Mindfulness meditation is perhaps the most common. Here, you actively focus on the sensations around you. Instead of letting your mind wander, you focus on how your bottom is connected with the floor, with any sounds going on around you. With this method, you can begin to appreciate how your spirit sits in your body, and it allows you a deeper connection with it.

To go one step further, you can deeply connect with the energy of the universe. Sitting comfortably, begin to imagine the energy that floats boundlessly above you entering the crown of your head. You can feel it surge down your spine, hitting every chakra on the way down. This energy courses through your fingertips and into every inch of your body, energizing you and preparing for re-entry into the world.

You can also ask for the wisdom to solve your worldly problems. Remember that our inner spirit already has all of the answers we are looking for. We are constantly forced to make decisions, and unless we are deeply connected with our inner spirit, it is easy to get off track.

Asking your inner self and the universal spirit for guidance is very easy. All you need to do is be present in the moment and ask. Remember that we must ask for things that are for the greater good, and not ultimately selfish. If you ask for the path that leads to the fancy car and the nice house, the universe will likely not have an answer for you. Asking for happiness and clarity is both helpful for you and for those around you, the greater good. If your intentions are pure, and you are asking to follow your destined path, you will find the answers you seek.

Don't expect to get the answers you need in one meditation session. Again, it takes practice to get reacquainted with your inner self. By practicing regularly and getting in touch with your spirit, you will gain wisdom and insight to better navigate through life.

No matter what type of meditation you decide to practice, continually grow and change. Your spirit is pure energy and is not bound by traditional barriers. Be regimented in choosing to practice daily, but do not limit your spirit to the same old meditation session. If you like to listen to music or soothing sounds, ask your spirit before you settle in what it wants to listen to. This may sound silly, but you have likely felt this feeling before.

You may feel that your basic routine is a little stale, but you press on because it is what you are 'supposed' to do. The feeling of boredom is something we have all felt, and this is a way of your spirit telling you that it needs something more. We may not always be able to listen, but when it comes to meditation, go ahead and give in to your spiritual desires. You will begin to make friends and better connection with your spirit, and it will reward you with happiness and wisdom.

If you are feeling that your spirit is dim and needs a bit of tender loving care, meditation is a great place to start. Physically taking the time to listen to your spirit and find out what it needs is the first step in healing. There are many situations in life that break our spirit and cause us to spiral out of control. We can use meditation to confront those feelings and walk through them with the help of the universal energy.

There is nothing in this world we cannot conquer with the power of meditation. If you are a bit skeptical of this practice, go ahead and give it a try. If nothing else, each session will leave you feeling relaxed and recharged in the moment. Continued practice and vigilance to the needs of your spirit will uplift you, and give you more ability to see the wisdom the universe has to show you.

CHAPTER 13
5-Minute Meditation

The goal of such a short meditation session is relaxation. This short sequence is great for reducing anxiety in the moment and clearing your head before diving back into your day. Enjoy!

Begin by finding a quiet, calm space. Take a seat in a comfortable position and slowly close your eyes.

Concentrate only on the sound of your breath as you exhale slowly and deeply. Now exhale gently, pushing all of the worries of the day out with each breath.

Pause.

Breathe in, soaking in the positive, calm energy from the room, and exhale all of the nervous energy within you. Feel it leave your body with every breath.

Pause.

Imagine your brain tidying itself up. It is closing all of the open files and storing them neatly away. As you breathe in, feel them closing, as you breathe out, they disappear from sight.

Pause.

Imagine your mind as a blank canvas, with only a light shade of tan strewn across the surface. It is ready to be painted. The canvas is clean and ready to accept new thoughts and brush strokes.

Pause.

Open your eyes, taking one last deep inhale. Now you are ready to resume your day. Your mind is fresh and clean, ready to work again. Go ahead in peace.

CHAPTER 14
15-Minute Meditation

Many things can be accomplished in a fifteen-minute meditation session. The mind can wander across the expanse of the universe in that time. This session will be devoted to exploring the far reaches of the mind, connecting with the universal spirit.

Find a comfortable position in a quiet room. Close your eyes and just be still.

Breathe deeply, in and out. With each exhale, feel your body propelling backward. Your breath is strong, capable of moving your spirit up and out of your body. Feel your spirit leaving your physical body, and hovering just above.

Each exhale pushes you further and further away from your body, up into the sky. You can see the tree tops inching away below you.

Pause.

Soon, the clouds look like tiny cotton balls, coating the earth's surface below you. As you exit the earth's atmosphere, the light fades away.

Pause.

Imagine you are looking down on the galaxy from above, watching the planets and stars swirling around each other. You can see and feel the energies flowing between them.

Pause.

You stop here for a moment, to take in the expanse of this universe, the ends at an unfathomable distance. You are swept up by the energy surrounding you, and a feeling of warmth courses throughout your spirit. You feel it in every extremity, slowly drifting through every finger and toe.

Pause.

This engrossing feeling immediately takes all of your worldly stress away, as you float weightlessly through the universe. As the energy consumes you, you are able to tangibly see every speck of energy that makes up the universe.

Pause.

You focus in on one energy path, recognizing each and every particle of energy that makes it up, much like a string of pearls.

Pause.

You feel overcome with wisdom, as you have now seen the inner workings of the universe, what you came here to recognize.

Pause.

You realize just how small your spirit is in comparison to the universal spirit. You feel connected to your very core to this higher energy, and you are stronger for it.

Pause.

Slowly, you drift back through time and space. You can see the earth begin to appear, at first a small circle, getting larger and larger.

Pause.

The clouds begin to reappear over the surface, your face feeling damp and refreshed as you pass back through them.

Pause.

The treetops begin to emerge, and you have reunited with your physical body yet again. Before re-entering, you hover there for a moment. You understand with newfound wisdom that this body is your temple. You rush back in, giving life and energy through every inch of it.

Pause.

You cleanse the body with your energy, removing all stresses, toxins, and worries. Your mind is clear and fresh, your body rejuvenated with this ethereal energy.

Pause.

You breathe new air into your lungs, as if for the first time. Slowly, you begin to awaken, ready again to join the earth.

Pause.

Your eyes awaken slowly, meeting the sun shining, the birds chirping, the sound of still and quiet. You are new again, ready to face the day with happiness, clarity, and wisdom. You are an irreplaceable being on this earth, and you carry on with a purpose.

CHAPTER 15
30-Minute Meditation

This thirty-minute session is meant to reboot your entire system. Feel the energy flow through you to completely rejuvenate your mind, body, and spirit. You will leave feeling ready to go and face the world. Enjoy!

Find a comfortable spot in a quiet place. Sit or lay down comfortably. Calm your breath, slowly inhaling and exhaling.

Pause.

Close your eyes and imagine that you are in a field of black eyed Susans. Together they make a field of yellow, with little black specks canvassing the surface.

Pause.

The field is bright and sunny, feel the warmth of the sun's rays on your face as it emerges from behind a puffy, white cloud.

Pause.

Feel the smile grow on your cheeks as the breeze whisks away your stress and emotions.

Pause.

Hear the breeze rustling through the flowers, touching on every petal. Hear the sounds of crickets chirping in between the leaves. They are so busy and you are so still.

Pause.

See the swallows flitting their wings just above the flowers. They sing and accept the energy from the sun as well. Everything is in perfect harmony at this moment.

Pause.

A small, half-grown black eyed susan catches your eye, just in front of you. It is much smaller than those around it, yet perfect just the same.

Pause.

You look at its face as the breeze gently tests its long stem. Each petal is perfectly symmetrical around its center, except for one. This is its imperfection, letting the universe know who it is, why it is special.

Pause.

Each petal is a bright golden yellow, with perfect, crisp edges and a bone down the middle. They stretch far out from the center as if reaching out toward its other flower companions.

Pause.

The dew from the morning still sits in the crevices of the flower, around its black center. Each droplet catches and reflects the light, bringing a jewel-like quality over the flower.

Pause.

You begin to hear a soft buzzing sound, slowly emerging from the distance. It circles around you. It is a honey bee, looking for the perfect flower.

Pause.

It hovers around a few flowers before landing gently and gracefully on the flower in front of you. The stem bends just slightly with the added weight.

Pause.

You turn your focus to this minuscule honey bee with its plump body and golden yellow hair. It looks soft to the touch underneath its luminescent wings. The bee is calm for a moment,

before attending to its work. It stops and drinks from the tiny water droplets coating the petals.

Pause.

You meet your breath with that of the bee, connecting on a spiritual level. You are both equally enjoying this flower, and that is all there is, frozen in time. For a moment this connection is powerful and strong. Just as quickly as it came, the bee pushes off the flower and disappears into the meadow.

Pause.

You focus your attention out back onto the field. You appreciate the stark contrast between the bright golden flowers and the blue sky as your backdrop. You continue to look around, unable to fully soak in the beauty of this scenery.

Pause.

Your eyes close, and all your senses focus on the sound of the crickets. Each chirp like a melody floating on in the background of your brain. All you feel is the warmth of the sun cascading over your shoulders. Everything is calm and focused in this moment.

Pause.

As you sit in that field, you feel your bottom connected with the earth. Feel the energy flowing up through the bottom of your spine. As you breathe in, accept this energy wholeheartedly from the earth.

Pause.

As you exhale, feel all of your negative energy flow out, as the earth accepts it. With each breath, you are renewed with a revitalizing energy. It can hardly be contained.

Pause.

You are refreshed, renewed, and you feel this new energy coursing through every inch of you. Through your spine, down to each and every finger tip.

Pause.

You are vibrating, your spirit ready to drive your physical body, ready to propel it forward.

Pause.

Open your eyes. Recognize where you are in your quiet space. Feel the energy coursing through your body, just as in the imagery. This energy is real. You have connected spiritually with this universal energy, and it is ready to propel you forward.

Take a few deep breaths, readying your body for movement. Now get up, and carry out your day using the energy the universe has given you. Do good with that energy.

CONCLUSION

Thank you for making it through to the end of *Spiritual Healing: Heal Your Life, Cleanse Your Body, Clear Your Mind, and Increase Mindfulness with Guided Meditation*. Let's hope it was informative and able to provide you with all of the tools you need to achieve your goals of achieving inner peace and healing your spirit.

The next step is to put some of these ideas into practice and start on your journey to spiritual wellness.

Finally, if you found this book useful in any way, a review on Amazon is always appreciated!

www.ingramcontent.com/pod-product-compliance
Lightning Source LLC
Chambersburg PA
CBHW071508070526
44578CB00001B/476